W9-BJH-932

An Imprint of Sterling Publishing
387 Park Avenue South
New York, NY 10016

This 2012 custom edition is published exclusively for Sandy Creek by QEB Publishing.

Edited, designed, and picture researched by
Starry Dog Books Ltd
Consultant Steven Downes, of the Sports Journalists' Association www.sportsjournalists.co.uk

ISBN 978-1-4351-4414-9

For information about custom editions, special sales, and premium and corporate purchases, please contact Sterling Special Sales at 800-805-5489 or specialsales@sterlingpublishing.com.

Manufactured in Guandong, China
Lot #:
2 4 6 8 10 9 7 5 3 1
09/12 .

CONTENTS

Ball and Stick Sports

Winter Sports

Extreme Sports

BALL SPORTS

There are lots of different ball sports you can try with your friends, like football and baseball. See if you can form a team! This chapter will focus on well-known, organized ball sports that you can try. Some of these, such as soccer and volleyball, are team sports; others, such as bowling, are more individual sports. All of them are fun and exciting to learn.

GETTING GEARED UP

In many ball sports, players come into contact with each other. Wearing protective gear around your head and body can prevent injuries if you bump into another player or if you fall over. This is why soccer players often wear shin guards, and football players wear helmets and shoulder pads.

All geared up in pads, gloves, and helmet, this young football player is about to throw the ball.

TAKE IT SLOWLY!

Before you run out of the door and start kicking, throwing, or spiking your ball of choice, it is important to keep a few things in mind. Remember, the **amateur** or **professional** players that you may follow are very experienced at what they're doing. Some of them are international champions in their sport, and have been practicing for years and years. Others are still amateurs, but have trained with professional **coaches** for some time. So don't expect to perform at the same levels or complete the same moves that they do! First you need to learn the basics of your chosen sport.

MASTERING THE GAME

Learning a new sport means understanding and mastering the basics. Why not form a club with your friends? Or you could find a club in your area. You'll need to take good care of your equipment and practice a lot. All sports, from basketball to bowling, keep you healthy and active. Remember to drink plenty of water, eat well, and take breaks whenever you need to.

KEEP SAFE

All sports involve a degree of danger, and some ball sports require more safety equipment than others. However, when they are played by the rules, they can all be fun and exciting to learn, so get ready for your new ball-sport adventure!

FOOTBALL

Football is a popular spectator sport throughout the world, but nowhere is it more closely followed than in the USA, where thousands of people enjoy watching high school, college, and professional games.

Young players in touch football need helmets to protect their heads and necks.

SIMPLE OBJECTIVE

The goal in football is simple: two teams of 11 players try to move the ball down the field and score points. Points are scored in many ways. A touchdown is worth six points. A touchdown is when the player moves the ball across the goal line, either by running with it or catching it from the **quarterback**. After a touchdown, the scoring team can get one extra point by kicking the ball through the goalposts.

TOUCH FOOTBALL

Touch or flag football is another version of the game. Instead of **tackling**, players just touch each other or pull a flag from their opponent's pocket. See if you can form a league in your neighborhood.

TACKLING

Football involves **tackling**, trying to knock other players down to stop them from moving down the field with the ball. For protection, players wear pads all over their bodies and a helmet. The quarterback needs a helmet that won't restrict his view because he has to spot who to throw the ball to or which **runner** to hand it to.

THROWING THE BALL

A football has pointed ends and is laced up. When you throw a football, your thumb should hold one end of the ball, and your fingers should line up with the white laces on top.

ALL IT TAKES!

Children can start playing organized football as young as eight years old. But at the most basic level, all you need for a game are two things: a football and someone to throw it to! If you want to try it out, the best place to start is in your yard, throwing passes to a friend.

A football player wears a special shirt, called a jersey, over his or her pads. The jersey may have the player's name and/or number on it.

THE PROS

In the USA and Canada, football teams play in professional **leagues**: the NFL (National Football League) or the CFL (Canadian Football League). These leagues are made up of teams that play each other throughout the season. The NFL season ends with the Super Bowl. The best CFL teams play for the Grey Cup.

The Super Bowl is the championship game played by the two top-ranking teams in the NFL. It is watched by at least 80 to 90 million viewers on TV in the USA alone, and is widely celebrated as a holiday, called Super Bowl Sunday.

The quarterback is often the leader of the team. He calls out coded signals to the other players to tell them what moves to make.

ACCURATE KICKING

In football, the job of the team's kicker is to kick the ball as far downfield as possible or to score by kicking the ball between the goalposts. Although this may look easy, kicking the ball accurately for 50 yards or more takes a lot of practice.

RUNNERS

Unlike soccer, in which most players need to run a lot, the amount of running in football depends on the position being played. The quarterback, for example, doesn't usually run with the ball very often, but a receiver, who runs down the field and tries to catch the ball that's being thrown by the quarterback, must be quick and agile.

At the start of play, the center (right, in a black headband) "hikes" the ball, meaning he or she passes it backward between his or her legs to the quarterback.

POWDER PUFF FOOTBALL

Don't think football is just for the boys! Girls can form their own teams, too. Powder Puff football is popular in high school, and the games are usually played to raise funds for charity. It's a version of flag football in which the defensive team stops the ball-carrier not by tackling her, but by removing a flag from a belt around her waist.

VOLLEYBALL

Volleyball can be played indoors on a court, or outside on the beach. Two teams stand separated by a high net. The aim of the **attacking** team is to hit the ball over the net and onto the ground on the other side. The **defending** team tries to hit the ball back over the net before it can touch the ground. Set up a net in your backyard and play with your friends!

THE SCORING SYSTEM

The first team to score 25 points (and be two points ahead) wins the set. The team that wins the most sets out of five wins the match. The fifth set is usually played to 15 or 30 points, depending on the league or level of the players. Set up a net in your backyard and play with your friends!

INDOOR VS. BEACH VOLLEYBALL

The rules and setup of indoor and beach volleyball are slightly different. In beach volleyball, two or more players make up a team, and players can wear swimsuits and sunglasses. In indoor volleyball, six players make up a team. They wear numbered shirts and protective knee pads.

Professional volleyball players often use an overhead serve, as seen here. If you are new to volleyball, an underhand serve is easier to learn.

SERVE, BUMP, SPIKE

The game starts with the attacking team **serving** the ball over the net. To keep it from hitting the ground, one of the receiving team will **set**, **dig**, or **bump** the ball, which means hitting it up into the air. His or her teammate can then attack by spiking the ball. This involves jumping up high and hitting it sharply downward back over the net.

The player on the right in this game of beach volleyball has spiked the ball over the net. The player on the left has tried, unsuccessfully to block.

BLOCKING THE BALL

The players receiving the spike try to block it, which means they **deflect** the ball before it hits the ground. Each team is allowed three hits to get the ball back over the net to the other team.

JUNIOR VOLLEYBALL

Many beach volleyball competitions are just for junior players. These championship games are usually divided into three age categories: under 14, under 16, and under 18. Many of the best junior players are from the USA, Australia, and Brazil.

BASKETBALL

Most young boys and girls love basketball. It's an easy game that requires only a basketball, a hoop, and lots of practice with your friends! Professionals, however, play on a large court with five players on each team, referees, uniforms, and strict rules.

TALLEST?

According to the *Guinness Book of World Records*, the tallest professional basketball player is Paul 'Tiny' Sturgess, who stands 7' 7.26" tall. English-born 'Tiny' now plays for the Harlem Globetrotters.

MOVING AROUND THE COURT

In a basketball game, players try to move the ball to the other end of the court. They can move it by dribbling (bouncing it up and down using their hands as they walk or run), **passing** (throwing or bouncing it to another player), or shooting (throwing it toward the basket). Simply carrying the ball is not allowed.

WOMEN'S OLYMPIC BASKETBALL

Men's basketball has been an Olympic sport since 1936, but women's basketball only became an Olympic sport in 1976. In recent years the women's medals have been dominated by the USA, Russia, and Brazil.

SCORING POINTS

An arch is marked on the court around the basket. If you shoot the ball from inside the arch and it goes in, you score two points. If you "make a basket" from outside the arch, you score three points.

In a professional game of basketball, once a player gets the ball, he or she must try to shoot a basket within 24 seconds. This is called the 24-second rule.

HOOP HEIGHT

In professional basketball, the rim of the basket is usually 10 feet from the ground. For children, the hoop height can vary according to age and ability. Some basketball hoops are designed so they can be raised or lowered.

ONE-ON-ONE

Playing basketball with just yourself and a friend is sometimes called "one-on-one." This is a fun and easy way to play basketball that allows you to practice shooting baskets and moving with the ball. You could even make up your own practice exercises, such as setting up a series of small cones and dribbling the ball around them.

Basketball is popular all over the world. These children are playing on a dirt court in the Kibera township in Nairobi, Kenya.

SHOOTING PRACTICE

In "one-on-one," if you shoot a basket and score, the other player **gains possession** of the ball. Before he or she can shoot, the player must first dribble the ball outside the key, a rectangular area in front of the basket. If you shoot a basket and miss, either of you can try to catch the ball as it comes off the backboard (the large white board behind the basket). However, you cannot score without first moving or dribbling the ball outside the key.

BALL AND BASKET FACTS

A basketball hoop is closely related in size to a basketball. Professional male basketball players play with a ball that measures about 29.9 inches in circumference (the distance around the ball). Women players use a ball about 29 inches in circumference. The rim of the hoop must be large enough to let the ball pass completely through. Basketballs for kids come in a range of sizes and weights. A coach will be able to choose the best size for your age and ability.

LEARN THE LINGO

Special names are given to different basketball shots. If you dribble up to the hoop and drop the ball right into the basket, it's called a "dunk shot." If you shoot and miss the basket completely, it's an "air ball." If you bounce the ball off the backboard and into the basket, it's called a "layup."

THE U.S. HALL OF FAME

The U.S. Basketball Hall of Fame, in Springfield, Massachusetts, is filled with basketball legends, history, and trivia. You can meet players and watch them perform on the center court, or have your photo taken beside the NBA (National Basketball Association) trophy.

SOCCER

Soccer is the most popular sport in the world. You may start by having a simple pass in the park with some friends, but before long you'll be wanting to play in the World Cup! In an organized game, soccer involves two teams of 11 players. The aim is to score more goals than the opposing team in 90 minutes.

THE REFEREE

The referee's job is to make sure the players follow the rules. If a player **fouls**, the referee blows a whistle, stops the game, and awards a penalty, if necessary.

DAVID BECKHAM

David Beckham, former England captain, may be the world's most famous soccer player, but it's not just because he plays so well! He is also a hugely popular celebrity, appearing in all kinds of different magazines and on TV talk shows.

THE TEAM

The players each have a position to play on the field. Defensive players tend to stay nearer their own goal to support the goalie. **Midfielders** do much of the tackling. They try to take possession of the ball from the opposing team and pass it to the **strikers**. The strikers are the ones who try to score goals! The goalie tries to stop any balls from getting into the net.

« If the referee holds up a yellow card, it warns a player that he or she has committed a foul. If the player commits a second foul, he or she is given a red card and taken out of the game.

GETTING IN SHAPE

Soccer involves a lot of running, so practice sessions are designed to build up your strength. You might warm up before a game with a quick jog. To practice quick moves, try running and kicking a ball around a line of cones.

SHIN GUARDS AND CLEATS

Soccer players wear shin guards under long socks to protect the fronts of their legs (below the knees) from kicks. They also wear special cleats to give them better grip on slippery or muddy fields.

HEADS UP!

Professional soccer players sometimes let the ball bounce off their heads in a move called a "header." Although it looks easy, it requires practice.

*Women's soccer is popular all over the world, and every four years professional women soccer players compete in the **FIFA** Women's World Cup.*

ONLY THE BEST

Soccer fans all over the world are enthusiastic supporters of the FIFA World Cup. In this famous competition, held every four years, national soccer teams from around the world compete to win the famous gold trophy. Millions of fans watch the **qualifying matches** on TV. The live games are played outdoors in front of thousands of spectators. The first men's World Cup was held in 1930, and the first women's World Cup was held in 1991. Why not watch the next World Cup with your soccer team?

LANDON DONOVAN

Landon Donovan is America's king of soccer. He plays for LA Galaxy. Not only is he the highest US scorer ever, but he made US World Cup history by playing at three different championships. He scored a grand total of five goals at the 2010 World Cup.

THE FAMOUS TROPHY

From 1930 to 1970, the winners were presented with the Jules Rimet trophy, named after the ex-FIFA president. In 1970, Brazil got to keep this cup after winning for the third time. It was replaced in 1974 by the FIFA World Cup.

Spain were winners of the 2010 World Cup and the first team to win outside of their home continent (Europe).

WORLD CUP FEVER

Since the first World Cup was held, millions of fans have lined up to cheer for their nation's team. Fans show their support in lots of creative ways: some paint their faces and bodies, dye their hair, or wear clothing in the colors of their country's flag. Fans also sing songs to support their team, and wave their national flags.

> *Many soccer players and audiences heard vuvuzelas for the first time at the 2010 World Cup in South Africa. The constant noise of the plastic horn-shaped instrument proved unpopular and even drowned out commentators!*

PELÉ

Pelé, whose full name is Edson Arantes do Nascimento, is considered by many to be the world's best soccer player ever. He started playing for the Brazilian national team at the age of 16, and during his 22-year playing career he scored 1,281 goals.

RUGBY

Rugby developed in the 1800s from a form of soccer that had been played at Rugby School in England since the 1600s. The game is now popular not just in the UK and Ireland, but also in France, New Zealand, Australia, and South Africa, among other countries. Why not try playing this exciting game with your friends?

THE RIGHT GEAR

If you want to play rugby, you'll need a pair of rugby shorts, a rugby shirt, a mouth guard, and a rugby ball. You'll also need a pair of cleats for grip. Some players wear padding and a helmet for extra protection.

HOW TO SCORE

Depending on the age of the players, the game can be played with 7, 10, 12, 13, or 15 players on a side. The aim is to move the ball to the other end of the field by carrying, passing, or kicking it. Once the ball is near the other team's **try line**, there are several ways to score points. A player can cross the try line and, while holding the ball in their hands, touch the ground with the ball to score a "try." Or he or she can **drop-kick** the ball over the crossbar between the opposing team's goalposts. (To read about the scoring system, see page 24.)

KICKING A GOAL

There are several ways to score a goal in rugby. After a team has been awarded a "try," one of the players on that team can try to get additional points by kicking the ball over the crossbar of the other team's goalposts. If successful, this is called a **conversion**. A **penalty kick** also earns the team points.

STARTING YOUNG

You can start playing American Flag Rugby at the age of five. Instead of tackling, players pull a flag from their opponent's pocket. Girls and boys can play together until the age of 14.

Catching an oval-shaped rugby ball can feel a little strange if you are used to a round ball. It's best to catch it with fingers spread apart, hands facing the ball, and elbows bent. Practice catching and throwing with your friends.

RUGBY CODES

There are two distinct "codes" of rugby: Rugby Union and Rugby League. Rugby Union is normally played with 15 players on the team. In Rugby League there are 13 players on the team. Why not try both and see which you like better?

POINT SCORING

The scoring systems are different in Rugby Union and Rugby League. In Rugby Union, a try scores 5 points, a conversion 2 points, and a **drop goal** 3 points. In Rugby League, a try scores 4 points, a conversion 2 points, and a drop goal 1 point.

TACKLING

To get the ball from an opposing player, players are allowed to tackle, or knock each other to the ground. This is what gives the game its rough-and-tumble reputation.

In rugby, you are allowed to run forward holding the ball.

THROWING THE BALL

In rugby, players are allowed to throw the ball to another player. However, they are not allowed to throw the ball forward! It can only be thrown to a player who is behind the ball-carrier, or to the side of them. It can, however, be kicked or carried forward.

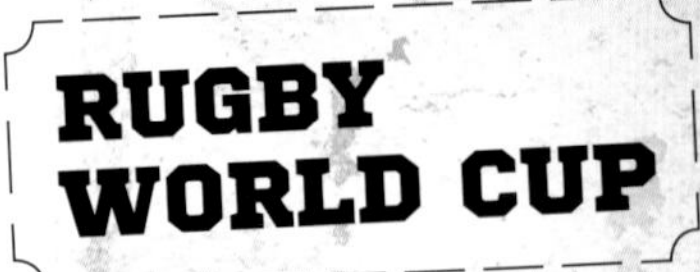

RUGBY WORLD CUP

According to some estimates, only the soccer FIFA World Cup and the Summer Olympics are more popular spectator sports than the Rugby World Cup! The first Rugby World Cup, played in 1987, was hosted by Australia and New Zealand. It is held every four years.

LEARNING THE LINGO

Rugby has a language all its own. A **scrum** is when eight players from each team group together against each other to restart the game. A **ruck** refers to a battle for possession of the ball once it has been dropped by a tackled player.

Sometimes the ball is kicked outside the playing area (this is called kicking the ball "into touch"). When this happens, players from each team stand in two lines, in a formation called a "line-out," and attempt to catch the ball when it is thrown in from touch.

HANDBALL

Handball is a team sport usually played indoors between teams of seven players. It is played at the Olympics. In the USA, this game is called team handball or European handball.

WORLD CHAMPIONS

The men's and women's team handball world championships are organized by the International Handball Federation (IHF). In 2012, the Norwegian women's team beat the French team (above).

TEAM HANDBALL

Team handball (European handball) is a fast, energetic sport in which the players may pass or dribble the ball in any direction. Players try to score on a soccer-like goal by throwing the ball from anywhere outside a 19.7-foot semicircle.

An outdoor American handball court has three walls. Indoor courts usually have four walls.

AMERICAN HANDBALL

American handball is played on a walled court. In a "singles" game, two players play against each other. In "doubles," there are two teams of two players. In singles, one player serves for points, dropping the ball to the floor and hitting it against the front wall. The other player receives the ball. A game is won by the first player or team to score 21 points, and the winner is the first player or team to win two out of three games. See if you can get a tournament going with your friends!

A LONG HISTORY

Although the game has changed a lot since ancient times, most historians agree that the Greeks and Romans played a version of handball. The game also has a strong tradition in Ireland, where a version called Gaelic handball is played.

In team handball, a player may hold the ball for only three seconds and may take only three steps with the ball.

BOWLING

There are many different kinds of bowling games. One of the best-known is ten-pin bowling, played indoors in a bowling alley. Another is lawn bowls, played outdoors on a flat, grassy bowling **green**. Both versions involve rolling a ball along the ground toward a target some distance away. Try them both with your friends!

LAWN BOWLS

The aim in lawn bowls is to roll your balls (known as bowls) along the ground to try and get them as close as you can to a small, white ball called the "jack." You need to knock your opponents' bowls out of the way with your bowls in order to get close to the jack.

Bowls travel in a slightly curved path because of the way they are shaped.

FAMOUS TEN-PIN BOWLER

Tomas Leandersson of Sweden is one of the best ten-pin bowlers in the world. He has captained the European ten-pin bowling team, which plays a team from the USA every October for the Weber Cup.

SKITTLES

A very old version of bowling is skittles, which is said to date back to the 14th century. It is played both indoors and outdoors. Indoor skittles is played in a skittle alley (from 21 feet to 29.5 feet long). The game involves trying to knock over nine pins using a wooden ball. Outdoor skittles, using a light, rubber ball, is a great game for children.

TEN-PIN AND CANDLEPIN BOWLING

Ten-pin bowling involves rolling a 15-pound bowling ball along a long, narrow lane toward a set of 10 pins,to knock over as many of them as possible. Candlepin bowling, which is played in parts of the USA and Canada, uses a smaller ball (about 2 pounds). You usually get at least two tries to knock down the pins.

ALLEYWAY

A bowling alley, where ten-pin bowling is played, is divided into many separate lanes so a lot of people can play at once. After you roll your ball down the lane, a machine returns it to you by way of a separate narrow channel. The fallen or remaining pins are automatically cleared away, and a new set of pins is set up for the next player.

▲ Players in a bowling alley often wear special bowling shoes, which have soles that don't scuff the surface of the lane.

BALL AND STICK SPORTS

In the world of sports, there are many different activities that use some type of bat (or stick) and ball. You might choose to hit tennis balls over a net with a racket, or you may enjoy learning how to sink balls with a pool cue. There's a bat and ball sport to suit every personality!

PLENTY OF CHOICE

If you like playing on a team, consider playing lacrosse or field hockey with your friends. If you prefer an individual sport, tennis may be the game for you. If you like fast action, try table tennis. If a slower pace with sudden spurts of activity is more your style, you could try baseball. Whatever sport you choose, they are all fun, easy to learn, and a great way to make new friends!

Some female lacrosse players wear cage-like face guards to protect their eyes during a game.

TIME AND PATIENCE

Before you head for the field, court, or course, there are a number of things to keep in mind. Remember that many of the players you see on TV or at live events are professionals with years of experience (and practice). So don't expect to be as good as they are right away! Learning any new sport takes time and patience, and it's best to focus on having fun, rather than trying to master every little detail of your chosen sport.

PROTECT YOURSELF

Many bat and ball sports require protective gear, such as helmets and pads, for the body or face. Such protective equipment for your head and body can prevent injuries if you bump into another player, are hit by a ball, or slip and fall down.

PRACTICE MAKES PERFECT

As any good coach will tell you, learning a new sport means understanding and mastering the basics. You'll need to take good care of your equipment and practice a lot. All sports, from golf to table tennis, keep you healthy and active. Remember to drink plenty of water, eat well, and take breaks whenever you need to. Most sports also involve a certain amount of danger. But when they are played correctly, they're all fun!

LACROSSE

Lacrosse is an exciting game that was invented by the Native American Iroquois tribe. The modern game is played by two teams of 10 (men) or 12 (women). The players use lacrosse sticks, called crosses, to move a hard rubber ball around a field. They use the mesh pockets at the ends of their sticks to scoop the ball off the ground and pass it to other players, who catch it and pass it using their sticks.

AIM OF THE GAME

Lacrosse is similar to soccer in that the players run back and forth trying to get the ball into the other team's goal. The attackers line up close to the opponent's goal and try to score. The defenders stay near their own goal to defend it from the other team's attackers. As in soccer, each team's goalie stays close to his or her goal to guard it from the other team's players.

WHAT IS HURLING?

Hurling is thought to be the oldest field game in Europe. It is an Irish game similar to lacrosse. The stick (or hurley) and ball (or sliothar) resemble those used in field hockey. Two teams of 15 players hit the ball on the ground or in the air, and a player can pick up the ball with his or her stick and carry it for four steps.

In polocrosse, two teams of six players play the game on horseback.

PROTECTIVE GEAR

In men's lacrosse, players wear helmets to protect their heads, and on their hands they wear large, padded gloves. In women's lacrosse, there is less physical contact. Players wear mouth guards and face guards but only the goalie wears a helmet and padding.

The French named the early lacrosse sticks "crosses," because they looked like a bishop's staff, called a "crosse".

DID YOU KNOW?

Lacrosse is played at the international level by 26 countries and the Iroquois Nationals. The Iroquois is a group of First Nations/Native Americans mainly from eastern Canada and the northeastern USA. They are the only First Nations/Native American team allowed to compete in an international sport.

TENNIS

Tennis is fun and easy to learn. All you need to play is a racket, a ball, a net to hit the ball over, and someone to play against. Tennis is played on a court, either indoors or outdoors. Get a group together for a tournament!

TENNIS TALK

You will need to buy, rent, or borrow a tennis racket if you want to play tennis. The "grip" is the area of the tennis racket that you hold onto, or grip. The "head" is the part of the racket that hits the ball. Strings across the head form a grid of netting off which the ball bounces.

It used to be that tennis clothing had to be white, white, and whiter. Today, however, tennis outfits have changed. It's not unusual to find tennis players wearing red, blue, pink, or even black outfits.

WHO'S WHO IN TENNIS

Because tennis is so popular, its best players are often well known. In the United States, Andy Roddick is widely recognized. Roger Federer of Switzerland is a multiple winner at major competitions, such as Wimbledon and the U.S. **Open** while Andy Murray of Great Britain won a gold medal at the London Olympics in 2012. Among female tennis players, sisters Venus and Serena Williams of the United States have many loyal fans.

Maria Sharapova was born on April 19, 1987 in Siberia, Russia. She is 6' tall, and is one of the world's best tennis players.

WHERE TO PLAY

If you want to learn tennis, there are many ways to do so, from group or individual lessons to tennis camp or tennis clubs. Tennis can be played outdoors on **asphalt**, clay, or grass courts, or indoors at a sports center. In some parts of the world, outdoor tennis courts are roofed over in the winter with stiff domes of plastic called bubbles so players can play all year round.

Tennis is often played in the summer on outdoor courts. Players wear shorts or short skirts and lightweight shirts to keep cool.

FAMOUS COMPETITIONS

Tennis is popular all over the world, and many people like to follow the game (and the players) by attending competitions such as the U.S. Open, the French Open, or the Australian Open. If you can't get to a live event, you can follow the action on television.

SINGLES AND DOUBLES

There are two main ways of playing tennis. In a singles game there are just two players, one on each side of the net. In a doubles game there are four players on the tennis court, a team of two (called a pair) on each side of the net. In both types of games, only one ball is hit back and forth. The court is marked with outer **sidelines** and inner sidelines. Doubles players can hit the ball to the outer lines and singles players use the inner ones.

RACQUETBALL AND SQUASH

The games of squash and racquetball are related to tennis. Both involve hitting a rubber ball around an indoor court. In tennis, if the ball is hit outside the court it is considered out of bounds, but in racquetball and squash you can hit the ball off the walls as well as the floor. Both sgamesl can be played as a singles game or a doubles game. See if there are any courts near you and play with your friends.

A racquetball is slightly larger than a squash ball, and the racquet has a shorter handle.

3 30
2 40

GAME, SET, MATCH

The scoring system in tennis is quite complicated. Tennis is played in a sequence of games that are scored using points. At least six **games** make up a **set**, and generally two or three sets (but it can be as many as five) make up a **match**.

BADMINTON BASICS

Badminton is similar to tennis, except everything is a different shape! The rackets are lighter, the court is smaller, the net is taller, and instead of hitting a ball back and forth, players hit a small cone called a "shuttlecock" or "bird." Badminton became an Olympic sport in 1992, when Indonesia, South Korea, and China won most of the medals.

TRY, TRY, AND TRY AGAIN...

If you are learning tennis, you will probably do lots of practice exercises to improve your skills. Your coach may stand close to the net, for instance, and send over practice balls for you to return. Another easy way to practice tennis is to hit the ball against a wall.

STOP AND START

Tennis is a game of movement. Because the ball can be hit anywhere on the court, you'll need to run after it. Learning to run after the ball and then slow down enough to hit it back over the net can take some practice.

When serving, the player stands behind the baseline, throws the ball up into the air, and hits it over the net into the service box diagonally opposite (marked by white lines on the ground).

TABLE TENNIS

Table tennis is a fast and exciting game in which two players use small paddles to hit a hard plastic ball over a low net strung across a table. The players take turns serving for two points in a row. The first player to get 11 points (with a two-point lead) wins the game. When the server hits the ball, it must bounce on the server's side of the net first and then on the opponent's side before it is returned. The game requires great speed, and is fun both to watch and to play!

DID YOU KNOW?

Table tennis has precise rules. The International Table Tennis Federation (ITTF) states an official table tennis ball must be white or orange and weigh 0.1 ounces.

Ping-pong is popular with children all over China. These schoolchildren from the Guangxi Zhuangzu region are playing on a table made from a piece of concrete, with a line of bricks for a net.

WHAT IS PING-PONG?

Ping-pong is another name for table tennis. It is the term generally used when the game is played just for fun by children. Most people agree that the name came from the "ping" and "pong" noises made by the ball in the days before paddles had foam cushions.

GETTING STARTED

To play table tennis you need a few basic pieces of equipment: a paddle (or racket), a ball, a net, and a table. In international competitions the net must rise exactly 6 inches above the table. At home you don't need to be so precise. Instead of a net you could use a piece of fabric, or even a row of tin cans!

World champion table tennis players come from all over. Many of the world's best players are from China and South Korea.

BASEBALL

Baseball is one of the most popular games in the United States. To play, you only need a ball, a bat, a glove (to catch the ball) and a few friends. You might also want a cap to keep the sun out of your eyes.

PITCHER AND CATCHER

Two teams of nine players take turns to bat. The **pitcher** throws the ball to the **catcher**. The catcher crouches behind the **home plate**. The batter tries to hit the ball so that he or she can run around the four bases and score runs.

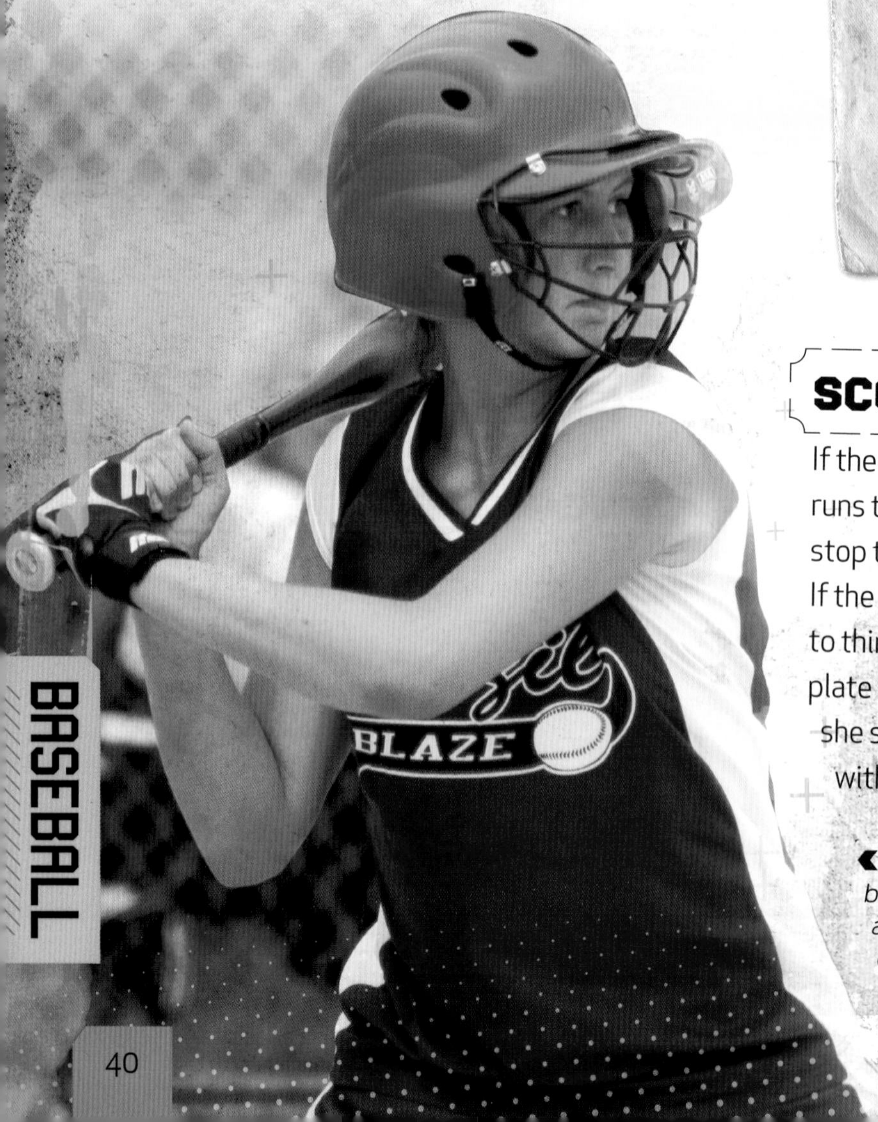

SCORING RUNS

If the batter hits the ball, he or she runs to first **base**. The batter can either stop there or run onto the next base. If the batter runs from first to second to third base and back to the home plate without being called out, he or she scores a home run. The team with the most runs wins.

Before taking a swing at the ball, the batter holds the bat at a 45 degree angle over his or her back shoulder.

THE FOUR BASES

The area of the field where the game is played is called the diamond. The corners of the diamond are marked by the four bases. Each base is guarded by a **fielder** called a **baseman**, who is ready to catch the ball. The pitcher stands in the center.

FIELDING POSITIONS

In an organized game, there are nine fielders. Inside the diamond are the pitcher, the catcher, four basemen, and the short stop (who fields between second and third base). Outside the diamond are the left fielder, the center fielder, and the right fielder.

This baseball game is being held at the Rogers Center in Toronto, Canada. It seats 49, 260 fans.

A GAME FOR EVERYONE

You can play baseball no matter how old you are, or whether you're a boy or a girl. If you like playing, you'll be fascinated by the history and culture that comes with it. In many parts of the USA, girls and boys play together on the same team. Some girls also play **softball**, a game similar to baseball, but with a larger ball. And very young children might play T-ball, a game in which you hit the ball off a T-shaped stand. Older children can move on to play baseball and softball games organized by the Little League.

You can take a tour or even have a birthday party at Yankee Stadium, home of the New York Yankees.

DID YOU KNOW?

Baseball may have developed in the mid-1700s from the English game **rounders**. In rounders, two teams take turns batting and fielding. The batter scores a "rounder" by running past each post before the fielders can touch the posts with the ball.

WORLD FAMOUS YANKEES

The New York Yankees are probably the best-known baseball team in the world. The reason? They have won the **World Series** 27 times! The World Series is a famous competition between the winners of the two leagues that make up Major League Baseball in the USA and Canada.

WORLDWIDE APPEAL

Baseball players from all over the world go to the USA to play. The Dominican Republic, Cuba, Japan, and Puerto Rico are all well known for their baseball stars. In the Dominican Republic, children play baseball on the streets. One of the most famous players in Major League baseball is Sammy Sosa, from the Dominican Republic.

➤ When batting, baseball players wear helmets to protect their heads. They also wear shoes with studs, which give good grip when they are running.

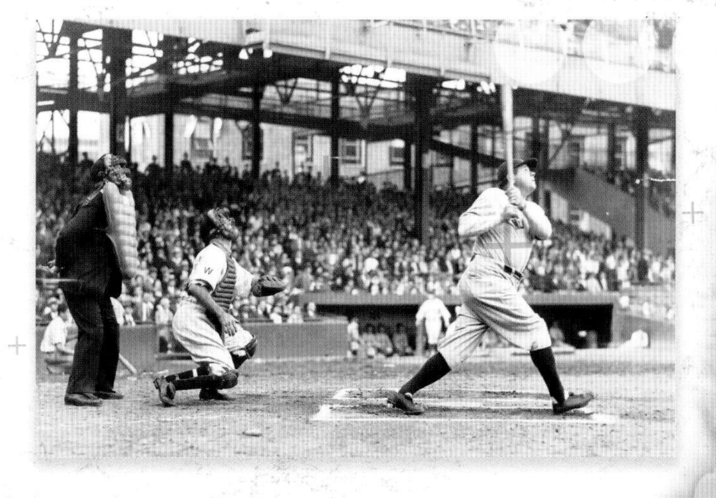

COOPERSTOWN

The U.S. Baseball Hall of Fame is in New York State. Take a trip to Cooperstown to learn about famous baseball players such as Joe DiMaggio and Babe Ruth (above). You can visit the hall of fame online at: www.baseballhalloffame.org

The game of golf involves using various clubs to hit a small ball into a set of 18 holes scattered around a course. Along the way are obstacles such as lakes, sand traps (bunkers), trees, and rough grass. The player who hits his or her ball into the 18 holes using the smallest number of strokes wins.

This man is using a putter to hit his golf ball into the hole, which is marked with a flag.

TALENTED TIGER

Tiger Woods is one of the world's best players. He has won many major golf tournaments, including the **Masters** four times, the British Open Championship three times, and the U.S. Open twice.

GOLF CLUBS

Golf players carry a variety of clubs, each designed for a different purpose. Most clubs can be grouped into one of three categories: **woods**, **irons**, or **putters**.

WHICH CLUB TO USE?

A player starts a game by hitting the ball for a long distance from a special area of the course called the tee. To hit the ball long distances, most people use a club called a "wood" or "driver."

As the player gets closer to the hole, he or she will probably use clubs called "irons." These are used for more accurate shots.

Once the ball is on the green, an area of very short grass where the hole is located, the player uses a "putter" to hit the ball into the hole.

WELL-KNOWN WOMEN GOLFERS

Golf is a great game for girls, some of whom go on to become top-earning professional women golfers. Michelle Wie did so when she was just 15 years old. Two other world-famous women golfers are Annika Sorenstam of Sweden, and Lorena Ochoa of Mexico.

Many golfers wear a glove on one hand to help them grip their clubs.

WORLDWIDE APPEAL

Golf has been played for at least 500 years in the UK, though its origins are uncertain. Today it is played all over the world on courses that use the natural environment, such as streams, lakes, hills, and trees, to add difficulty to the golfer's game. But it can be played anywhere. It was even played on the Moon, where astronaut Alan Shepard, on lunar mission Apollo 14, played a shot that he said went for "miles and miles" because of the low gravity!

MINIATURE GOLF

You might also enjoy miniature golf. The player uses a putter to move the ball through and around various obstacles, such as model windmills, in as few strokes as possible.

WHERE TO LEARN GOLF

There are many places to learn golf. Many large golf courses offer junior lessons. There are also golf clubs, golf camps, and golf outings to choose from. Most golf courses have a resident pro, or golf expert, who will give advice to new players.

*On a **driving range**, golfers spend many hours practicing how to stand and how to hold and swing the club to hit the ball.*

EXTRA EQUIPMENT

Golfers wear special gloves to provide grip and shoes with spikes to stop them from slipping as they take shots. In their bag they also need golf balls and "tees." A tee is a small, Y-shaped piece of wood or plastic on which the ball sits when the player strikes the ball (tees off) at the start of each hole.

Having hit the ball, the player "follows through" with a swing.

DID YOU KNOW?

Some golf courses that are next to the ocean are called "links." One of the most famous is Pebble Beach (left) in California. It overlooks the Pacific Ocean. In Ireland, Ballybunion is beside the Atlantic.

FIELD HOCKEY

Field hockey in its modern form was first played in the mid-1700s by schoolchildren in England, and it is still popular with children. The game usually takes place on a rectangular field, where players are arranged in similar positions to those on a soccer field. There are attackers, defenders, and a goalkeeper. Using wooden sticks, the players pass the ball up and down the field and try to hit it into the other team's goal.

A TEAM GAME

There are 11 players on a field hockey team. As in soccer, passing, marking, and tackling are important aspects of the game. The field hockey stick itself is just under 3.3 feet long. It is similar to an ice hockey stick, but the head, the area used to hit the ball, is smaller.

OLYMPIC ALL-STAR

Field hockey has been part of the summer Olympic Games since 1908. One of the most successful players of all time is Rechelle Hawkes (above) of Australia. She has won three Olympic gold medals.

A penalty corner is a type of play that allows one team to try and score from near the goal. They get this chance because the other team has fouled. Five players from the defending team must stand behind the back line until the ball has been hit.

FIELD FACTS

Most outdoor field hockey is played on artificial turf fields that measure 100 yards long by 60 yards wide. The goal at each end is 7 feet high and 12 feet wide. Around the goal there is a D-shaped area known as the **shooting circle**.

STICK FACTS

The head of a field hockey stick has a rounded side and a flat side. The flat side is used to hit the ball.

Players try to get the ball off their opponents. They are only allowed to hit the ball with the flat face of the stick.

BASIC EQUIPMENT

If you want to play field hockey, you'll need shin guards, a stick, and a ball. The shin guards are to protect your lower legs from the impact of the ball or another player's stick. In schools, field hockey is often played on grass, so cleats provide grip. At recreation centers and elsewhere, however, synthetic surfaces are more popular and sneakers should be worn. Some field hockey players also wear mouth guards to protect their teeth and goggles to protect their eyes.

STREET HOCKEY

Street hockey is closely related to field hockey and ice hockey. It is basically the same game, but is played on paved surfaces such as a street or rollerblading **rink**. The players wear sneakers or rollerblades, and use ice hockey sticks instead of rounded sticks.

There can be as many as ten players in a street hockey team, but ten of them will be ***reserves****. Only six members of the team take part in the action at any one time.*

A flying field hockey ball travels fast and is very hard, so the goalkeeper protects his or her body and face with extra padding and a helmet.

INDOOR HOCKEY

In indoor field hockey, the number of players, the rules of the game, and the size of the field are all different from outdoor field hockey. Instead of 11 players on a team, there are 6. The players cannot hit the ball, as in outdoor field hockey. Instead, they push, scoop, or flick the ball into the goal.

POOL

Pool is played on a rectangular table with pockets at the four corners and in the middle of each long side. Sixteen balls are used: seven red ones, seven yellow ones, one black one, and a white **cue ball**. Sometimes, players use seven solid-colored balls (numbered 1 to 7), the black 8-ball, and seven striped balls (numbered 9 to 15). Using a stick called a cue, the player hits the white cue ball, which in turn knocks one of the other balls into a pocket.

WHAT IS SNOOKER?

Snooker is similar to pool, but is played with 22 balls: 15 red ones (worth 1 point each when sunk) and six other-colored ones. They are yellow (worth 2 points), green (3 points), brown (4 points), blue (5 points), pink (6 points), and black (7 points), and a white cue ball. To score, players must "pocket" all the red balls first, then the colored balls. The black ball is sunk last.

CUE CLUES

A cue is usually made of wood and is slightly thicker at one end. The narrow end has a leather tip and is used to hit the white cue ball. Most pool players use chalk on the tip to improve contact between the stick and the ball.

Chalking the leather tip of a pool cue helps the player hit the ball with greater accuracy.

WHOSE TURN?

The players have one set of balls each, either a color (the reds or yellows), or the solids or stripes. They each try to sink all their balls into the pockets before the other player. If a player sinks the correct ball, he or she has another turn. If he or she fails to sink a ball, the opponent has a turn. In most games, the black ball must be sunk last.

➤ To judge what angle and strength to hit the cue ball, it helps to look down the length of the cue so you can line up your shot.

THE SPORT OF KINGS?

Many famous rulers, including Mary, Queen of Scots, and Napoleon Bonaparte, loved playing billiards (from which snooker and pool were developed).

WINTER SPORTS

The first snowboard, called the snurfer, was developed in the 1960s. The idea came from joining two skis together.

THE winter sports that are grouped together here are usually done in places where there is plenty of snow and ice. Some can be done all year long, such as ice skating (in an indoor rink) or downhill skiing (on **artificial snow**), but for the most part, the sports are meant to be done outside. Find out if there's a rink or mountain near you so you can go along with friends.

SNOW TIME!

Some winter sports, such as snowboarding and downhill skiing, are especially fun to do just after a heavy snowfall! Skating and ice hockey, of course, require ice. And cross-country skiing and **snowmobiling** can be done on just a few inches of snow.

REMEMBER TO TAKE IT SLOWLY!

Before you take up any new sport, it is important to remember that the professionals you see performing on television are very experienced and have been practicing for years. So don't expect to be able to do the same moves or go as fast as they do, without first learning the basics of your chosen sport.

SAFETY FIRST

You'll notice that most children wear helmets when snowboarding, downhill skiing, or playing ice hockey. Helmets provide protection for the head if you fall. Ice hockey also requires lots of body padding for protection against flying **pucks**, raised sticks, and other players. Different sports need different gear, and wearing the right protective gear will help keep you safe!

COACHING TIPS

As any good coach will tell you, learning a new sport means understanding and mastering the basic skills, taking good care of your equipment, and practicing a lot. All winter sports, from sledding to ski jumping, are part of a healthy and active lifestyle . Form a club with your friends or find one in your area. Remember to drink plenty of water, eat well, and take breaks whenever you need to.

SNOWBOARDING

Snowboarding is a relatively new sport. It involves riding a special board down a snow-covered hill or mountain. Since becoming an Olympic sport, snowboarding has become much more popular.

RIDING THE BOARD

A snowboard is larger than a **skateboard**, but smaller than a surfboard. To ride the board, you stand on it sideways wearing snowboard boots, which fit into **bindings** that hold the boots to the board. Snowboarders wear all the usual warm winter gear, snow pants, warm coat, gloves, and often goggles to protect their eyes from the glare of the sun.

REACHING THE TOP

To get up big hills, snowboarders use a lift. On some, you stand on your board while the lift pulls you up the hill. On others, you sit in a chair (a chairlift, above) or ride in a gondola (an enclosed cabin) and are carried up the hill.

SENSE OF BALANCE

Snowboarding requires good balance. You need to be able to shift your weight to stay upright as you move along, especially when moving fast. When you first learn to snowboard, you'll probably fall down a lot. This is normal!

BOARD AND BOOTS

Professional snowboarders generally wear hard boots that are a little like downhill ski boots. Some professionals prefer to use an Alpine snowboard, which is stiffer and narrower than a normal board.

Snowboarding is very popular with young people. From age 15 upward, both boys and girls can take part in the Winter Olympics.

STARTING OUT

If you want to try snowboarding, you could buy a simple board that can be used with standard winter boots. Instead of placing your feet into bindings, you slide the front of your boots under loop-like devices. This type of snowboard is great for beginners because if you lose your balance and fall over, your feet just fall out of the loops.

WHERE TO SNOWBOARD

Anywhere that's suitable for skiing or sledding is also suitable for snowboarding. But be sure to watch out for other people and trees that might be in your path! More advanced snowboarders can visit a snowboard park (also called a **terrain** park). Some terrain parks are stand-alone, meaning they are only designed for snowboarders. Others are part of a larger resort that has separate areas for downhill skiers and snowboarders on the same mountain.

TERRAIN PARK OBSTACLES

Terrain parks have small hills that snowboarders ride or jump over. These parks also have rails, which snowboarders slide down. In an event called snowboard cross, snowboarders race down a course. The fastest snowboarder wins!

To slide down a terrain park rail, you need to have excellent balance and plenty of experience.

SNOWBOARD LINGO

Snowboarding has a language all its own. The terms vary depending on where you're snowboarding. In the USA, to "roll down the windows" means to swing your arms wildly in the air in an attempt to catch your balance. "Huckers" are snowboarders who fling themselves through the air, but do not land on their feet.

INTERNATIONAL CHAMPIONS

Many of the medal-winning snowboarders come from snowy countries such as Sweden, France, Germany, and Canada. Shaun White from California won gold in the halfpipe event at both the 2006 and 2010 Winter Olympics.

SNOWBOARD SAFETY

If you are just learning to snowboard, don't be tempted to go down steep hills or over jumps too soon. It is far better to start slowly and learn the sport carefully than to end up with an injury.

HALF PIPE

Professional snowboarders compete in various kinds of competitions. One takes place on a feature called a half-pipe, a long, smooth channel in the snow. It looks like a tube that's been cut in half lengthways. In the men's and women's half-pipe event, experienced snowboarders perform jumps, flips, and other moves along the edge of the half-pipe or inside it.

HISTORY OF SNOWBOARDING

Snowboarding has only been around for about 50 years. It could have been started by a skateboarder who took off his wheels, or a surfer who used a **boogie board** in winter. But it most likely started with someone binding two skis together.

The Alley Oop trick is only for the most experienced snowboarders. It involves doing a 180-degree turn in midair above the lip, or top edge, of the half-pipe.

DOWNHILL SKIING

Downhill skiing (also called Alpine skiing) is a fun sport. The aim is to ride your skis downhill, making turns, going over small bumps, and feeling the wind in your face. When you ski, you balance yourself on two skis. You need to keep your skis next to each other and pointing in the right direction. This can take some practice, so don't be surprised if you fall over a few times!

EQUIPMENT

To try downhill skiing, you'll need a pair of skis and ski boots, which attach to the skis with metal bindings. It's also helpful to have poles to help push yourself along or steer your way downhill. For warmth and safety, it's best to wear a warm ski jacket and pants, a hat, gloves, a helmet, and eye protection, such as goggles or sunglasses.

For young skiers, like this three-year-old, a moving carpet is a great way to be carried up a small hill.

GOING UP!

If you are skiing at a ski resort, you will probably take a lift up the mountain. On some lifts, you keep your skis on and the lift pulls or carries you up the hill. If you ride in a gondola (an enclosed cabin) you take your skis off and sit or stand for the ride up the mountain. Some ski resorts have a "moving carpet," a large, flat **conveyor belt** that carries you up a slope with your skis on. At the top, you step off the moving carpet and ski back down the hill.

GENTLE SLOPES

If you are a beginner, you will probably learn to ski on a small hill (called a bunny hill), where you can get used to the feeling of wearing ski boots and moving around on skis. As you progress, you can move to a steeper hill or **trail**.

DID YOU KNOW?

Mountain ranges all over the world have been used for downhill skiing. Among the most famous are the Swiss Alps in Switzerland, where you can find ski resorts such as Davos, St. Moritz, and Wengen. There are other famous ski resorts in the Andes, the long mountain range that runs down the west coast of South America, as well as in the USA and Canada.

Most skiers wear sunglasses to protect their eyes from the sun reflecting off the snow, or goggles to protect their eyes against wind and snow.

OLYMPIC EVENTS

Downhill skiing is fun to do, and it's also very exciting to watch! The Winter Olympics feature a number of different events that involve downhill skiing. Some are races in which skiers ski down a mountain as fast as they can. In other events, skiers are judged on their ability to ski over bumps (called **moguls**) or perform difficult maneuvers (freestyle).

FREESTYLE

In a freestyle, or **aerial**, skiing event, a skier skis down a ramp that sends him or her up into the air. The skier then has three or four seconds to perform tricks, such as flips, twists, and spirals. Judges watch how well the skier lands and determine the difficulty of the maneuvers performed in the air.

RACES

There are many different kinds of downhill ski races. In a **slalom** race, skiers race downhill making tight turns around a set of skinny, flexible poles called slalom poles. The poles are stuck in the snow along the track. The skier who skis down the course the fastest, without missing any poles, wins the race.

The Olympic "combined" event includes one downhill and two slalom runs in one day.

SKI RESCUE

If a skier at a resort falls and gets hurt, he or she may be rescued by the ski patrol. These experienced skiers ski around all day looking for people who need help. Sometimes helicopters are used to rescue skiers from the highest mountains.

DOWNHILL

In an event called the downhill, skiers race one at a time down a steep, winding course as fast as they can. The skier who gets to the bottom the fastest is the winner. Downhill racers wear padded ski outfits. Skiers' outfits fit close to their bodies in order to make them more **aerodynamic**. The pads, as well as their helmets, protect them in case they fall.

ARTIFICIAL SNOW

Ski resorts that don't get enough real snow may use snow machines to make artificial snow.

American Lindsey Vonn has won four overall World Cup skiing championships (2008, 2009, 2010, and 2012).

SKATING

Skating is a fun sport in which you wear ice skates to move quickly across ice. Skates are special boots with sharp blades on the bottom. People skate on frozen ponds and lakes in winter or on indoor or outdoor skating rinks. Some people skate just for fun! Others master all kinds of difficult maneuvers that they perform in front of judges in skating competitions.

SKATE FACTS

Skaters can choose different types of skates depending on their skill or the kind of skating they want to do. (Check out www.isu.org for information about different kinds of skating.) Beginners wear basic recreational skates, while professional skaters wear skates specially made to fit their feet.

FIGURE SKATING

In figure skating competitions, skaters perform twirls, flips, and jumps, usually to music. Figure skaters at the Winter Olympics are judged on how well they perform their maneuvers, how difficult the moves are, and how well they skate with their partners. There are singles competitions for solo men and women skaters, pairs skating, and ice dancing.

In this figure skating move, called a death spiral, the man holds the woman's hand and pulls her in a circle around him.

BALANCING ACT

Skating requires good balance. You need to support the weight of your entire body on two very thin pieces of metal. If you are a beginner, you should expect to fall down a lot! Also, you may get sore ankles because they have to work hard to keep your feet at the right angles. Take lessons with some friends so you all learn together!

SKATING SAFETY

Never skate on a frozen lake, pond, river, or stream that has not first been checked for safety by an adult. While the ice may look thick enough to skate on, it may not be strong enough to hold your weight. Streams can be particularly dangerous because the water moving under the ice may prevent the ice from freezing completely. It's always safer to skate on a rink.

These kids are having a friendly speed-skating race. Speed skating is also an exciting Winter Olympic sport, in which skaters race around an oval-shaped rink.

DID YOU KNOW?

The machine that cleans the ice at a skating rink is called a Zamboni. It is named for Frank Zamboni, its inventor.

ICE HOCKEY

Once you know how to skate, you may want to learn how to play ice hockey. Ice hockey is a fast-paced, exciting game played on ice with sticks and a puck. A puck is a hard, smooth disc that glides easily across the ice. The aim is to hit the puck into the goal more often than the other team. The team with the most goals wins.

OLYMPIC RIVALS

Ice hockey is a popular Winter Olympic sport. Rivalry between Finland, the USA, Russia (above, in red, playing Slovakia), and Norway is legendary. At the 2010 Winter Olympics, Canada won gold in the men's and the women's events.

THE STICK

The bottom part of a hockey stick is called the blade. The blade is used to push the puck along the ice. Some ice hockey players wrap tape around the ends of their sticks to give them better grip on the puck.

In ice hockey, the referee wears skates to keep up with the action and to stay out of the way!

GAME BASICS

There may be up to 22 players on an ice hockey team, but only six play at one time. One of them is the goalkeeper, two play defense, and three are **forwards**. The action is so fast-paced that players are substituted every few minutes. Hockey is played on a rink, marked with colored lines painted beneath the ice.

STAY SAFE

Ice hockey players hit the puck very hard, which can cause it to fly into the air. If you've ever watched an ice hockey game, you may have noticed the clear, reinforced-plastic partitions that separate the fans from the players. These are designed to prevent pucks from flying into the crowd.

EQUIPMENT

To play ice hockey, you'll need skates, a helmet (often with a cage across the front to protect the face), gloves, padded pants, a stick, and shin, shoulder, and elbow pads. For more information about ice hockey, check out: www2.nhl.com/kids

With his wide leg pads, the goalkeeper blocks much of the goal when he stands in front of it. The forward has to aim carefully before shooting the puck.

DID YOU KNOW?

If an ice hockey player breaks the rules, he or she may be sent to the **penalty box** to sit out the action for a little while.

SLEDDING

Sledding is probably the easiest winter sport to try. All you need is a snow-covered hill and a sled of some kind.

SLED TYPES

Sleds come in many shapes and sizes. On an old-fashioned toboggan, several people can sit together, one behind the other. A flying saucer, on the other hand, is meant for just one person. It resembles cartoon drawings of **UFO**s from outer space!

DOG SLED RACE

In Alaska, sleds pulled by teams of dogs compete in the Iditarod Trail Sled Dog Race. Competitors in this annual race travel more than 1,000 miles over snow and ice.

LOOK OUT BELOW!

The first place you are likely to try sledding is in your yard (if it has a hill) or in a park. The hill doesn't have to be big. It's important that you can see the bottom of the hill from the top, so you don't bump into anything on the way down. (You'll need to ask permission if you want to sled on someone else's property.)

Many modern sleds, like this flying saucer, are made of plastic and have handles to hold onto.

STAYING WARM

You'll need to dress warm for sledding: thick pants, a coat, mittens or gloves, and a hat (or helmet). Don't forget to take a thermos full of hot chocolate to warm you up and a snack to give you energy to walk back up the hill.

This toboggan has two runners with a raised seat in between. The person in front holds onto the sled, and the person in back holds onto the person in front.

SLEDDING WITHOUT SNOW

Just because some people live in parts of the world where there isn't much snow, doesn't mean they can't enjoy sledding! On the islands of Hawaii, children ride banana tree stumps down grassy hills. For an extreme version of sledding, the ancient Hawaiians rode wooden sleds down hills of hardened **lava**.

SLEDDING EVENTS

If you like sledding, you may also like watching sports that involve sleds. At the Winter Olympics there are several events in which athletes ride a sledlike device down a hill, usually at very high speeds. The sleds have some unusual names: there's the two- or four-person bobsled, the **luge**, and the skeleton.

FEARLESS AND FAST

In the skeleton event, one person lies on a small sled and rides head first down an ice track. The aim is to reach the bottom in a faster time than the other competitors. In the luge competition, one or two riders lie on their backs on the luge and speed down the track feet first. The riders grip handles on the edge of the luge, which helps them steer.

SNOW TUBING

If you are attracted to the idea of bobsledding, a good place to start might be with a very fast form of sledding called snow tubing. A snow tube is an inflated rubber ring that you sit on. The air provides a cushion between you and the ground, so the ride doesn't feel too bumpy!

WHAT TO WEAR

All bobsled, luge, and skeleton athletes wear helmets to protect their heads and faces. They also wear tight racing suits to make their bodies more aerodynamic.

British athlete Amy Williams speeds down the skeleton track to win gold at the Winter Olympics in 2010.

At the start of a four-man bobsled race, the teammates reach a speed of about 25 mph before they jump on board.

BOBSLEDDING

In the bobsled event, two or four riders sit one behind the other in a special sled. At the start of the race, the teammates push the bobsled to get it moving and then leap on and sit down. The bobsled races down a narrow, twisting ice track. Tracks are usually about 1,312 to 1,531 yards long. The bobsled reaches speeds of up to 81 mph. The team that makes it to the bottom in the fastest time wins!

CROSS-COUNTRY SKIING

Cross-country skiing is just what it sounds like: wearing a pair of skis to travel across country (rather than down a hill). You use two poles to stay balanced and to help push yourself along. Trails or tracks for cross-country skiers may wind through woods and across frozen lakes and fields.

CLASSIC STYLE

The classic style of cross-country skiing is the easiest to learn. You place your skis side by side, about 6 inches apart. Then slide one foot forward at a time, as if you were walking without taking your feet off the ground. Gradually the walking action will turn into skiing.

WHERE TO SKI

In some parts of the world, such as the USA, Canada, and northern Europe, you can ski on special trails, which are wide, flat areas of snow that have been prepared for skiing. Some people prefer to make their own trail, making a path across the countryside (above), and then spend the night in a tent. Brrr! Perhaps there is a place near you where you can ski with your friends? Don't forget to ask permission if you want to ski across someone else's property.

GOOD EXERCISE

Cross-country skiing is very good exercise because it uses many of the big muscles in your body, including your arms and legs. Most cross-country skiers don't wear bulky winter gear, but instead wrap up in layers of warm clothing that can be removed (or put back on) as the body heats up (or cools down).

SKIS

For cross-country skiing you will need a pair of cross-country skis, which are very long and narrow, a pair of boots, and some poles. The boots are attached to the skis, but generally only at the toes. You lift your heels as you move along.

When you are cross-country skiing, you use poles to provide balance and to prevent a fall.

DID YOU KNOW?

In Finland, during the Winter War of 1939, some of the Finnish army wore cross-country skis while fighting the Russians.

Many people cross-country ski along paths that are used for hiking in the summer. If you are planning a long ski trip, bring food and drink to help give you energy.

RACING FOR PROFESSIONALS

At the professional level, there are several types of cross-country ski races. In some events, skiers use the classic style of skiing; in others they "skate" along the snow (moving their skis from side to side in order to go faster).

THE BIATHLON RACE

Cross-country skiing may date back to prehistoric times, when some people wore skis to hunt animals. This may explain the winter sport of biathlon, which combines cross-country skiing with rifle shooting.

DID YOU KNOW?

Skijoring is a sport that combines cross-country skiing with dogs (or sometimes horses). The skier is pulled along by the animals.

JUNIOR RACES

In northern Europe and Canada, children compete in the same types of cross-country ski races as adults. In a sprint-style race, you ski as fast as you can from one point to another. In a pursuit race, you start out doing one style of skiing (such as classic, sliding one foot forward and then the other), then stop halfway through the race, change to a second set of skis, and finish the race using the freestyle, or skating, style of cross-country skiing.

Competitors in cross-country ski races, like these children in Oslo, Norway, wear numbered bibs so the judges know who's who.

SNOWSHOE FACTS

In snowshoeing, you clomp through the snow wearing large, oval snowshoes. Old-fashioned snowshoes were made of wood and string; modern ones are made of lightweight metal and plastic.

LONG-DISTANCE AND RELAY RACES

Sweden has a race called the Vasaloppet, in which athletes ski for 56 miles. It is considered by some to be the longest, oldest, and largest cross-country ski race in the world. In contrast, in ski relay races, four skiers in a team each ski a distance of 6.2 miles for men and 3.1 miles for women. The team that completes the course first wins!

A competitor in a women's relay race at the cross-country skiing World Cup. In a relay, skiers take turns on the course.

SKI JUMPING

Ski jumping is a sport performed in competitions by highly experienced athletes. The skier skis down a long, steep slope with bent knees and his or her body close to the skis. This helps build up speed. From a ramp at the bottom, he or she launches into the air and leans forward so the body is almost parallel with the skis.

THREE STYLES

At the professional level, there are three ski jumping events: normal hill, large hill, and team events. The best ski jumpers reach distances of 110 yards off the normal hill, and can fly through the air for 142 yards off the large hill. After sailing through the air, the skier lands at the bottom of the hill. Points are scored for distance, and extra points are given for style and form.

SKI JUMPING EQUIPMENT

The skis used in ski jumping are longer and wider than those used in downhill or cross-country skiing. The shape of the skis helps the jumper sail through the air. Professional ski jumpers wear helmets and close-fitting suits.

From the top of this hill, the ski jumper can see the ramp at the bottom and the ski resort in Lillehammer, Norway, in the distance.

OLYMPIC GOLD!

Simon Ammann of Norway won double gold in ski jumping at both the 2002 and 2010 Winter Olympics.

Ski jumping is a great sport to watch live or on televison. However, if you want to try it, first you need to learn how to downhill ski. Then learn how to do small jumps. Gradually, with lots of practice and the help of a coach, you can build up to doing bigger jumps. When you are comfortable with jumps, you could have a friendly competition with your friends to see who can go the highest.

Practicing jumps on small hills is a good way to get the feel of flying through the air.

CANADIAN CHAMPION

Fourteen-year-old Trevor Morrice of Canada won the 2006 North American Junior Ski Jumping Championships. Trevor finished with 246.5 points on the K90 hill. The term K90 refers to the distance between where the skier leaves the jump (the takeoff) and the part of the hill where it starts to flatten out (called the **K point**). On a normal hill the distance is 98 yards, which is 90m, hence the name K90.

SNOWMOBILING

A snowmobile is a motorized sled powered by a gas engine. It has one central, **caterpillar track** and skis instead of wheels. To drive it, you sit on the back like you would on a motorcycle. Snowmobile racing is very popular. People race snowmobiles downhill, across country, and around ice tracks.

SLEIGH RIDING

Before the snowmobile was invented, people in snowy places often traveled by horse-drawn sleigh. Today, sleigh riding is a popular tourist activity in ski resorts and towns in snowy countries, such as Russia.

*Some snow cats are used on ski mountains, some are used to transport people or goods in snowy parts of the world, and others are used to explore the **Arctic** region.*

SNOW CATS

Snow cats are large snow vehicles used for "grooming" ski trails. Running on caterpillar tracks, they pull along a bar-shaped device that flattens or smooths out the snow.

BE CAREFUL!

If you want to try snowmobiling, you'll need warm-weather gear, thick pants, a warm coat, gloves, and boots, as well as a helmet. Some snowmobiles are designed for two people. The passenger sits behind the driver and holds onto two side handles. Snowmobiles can go very fast, but unless you are experienced, it's best to keep your speed low and to always have adult supervision.

‹ Snowmobiling is best in good weather conditions, when you can clearly see the trail ahead of you.

IRON DOG

The longest snowmobile race in the world takes place in Alaska and is called the Iron Dog. Competitors race a distance of more than 1,971 miles.

EXTREME SPORTS

The term "extreme sport" means many things to many people. For children, however, it usually means cutting-edge sports such as skateboarding, surfing, IronKids (triathlon), and mountain biking. The term became widely used beginning in 1995, when the sports channel ESPN launched the Extreme Games (later changed to the **X Games**), an international competition for more unusual, exciting sports.

Rock climbing is a little like learning to ride a bike because once you have learned the basics, you'll never forget them!

TRENDY, BUT NOT NEW!

Most of the extreme sports in this book have a modern reputation, but some have been around for a very long time. Surfing and kite surfing, for example, are actually thousands of years old, while mountain biking and kneeboarding are child-friendly versions of adult sports (**motocross/BMX** and waterskiing).

PROTECTIVE GEAR

You'll notice that people who you see climbing vertical rock faces, performing "ollies" in a skate park, or kayaking down rushing rivers always wear protective gear. You'll usually see them with a helmet, pads, ropes, life jackets, and the like. The right gear is important because many extreme sports lift you into the air, and wearing protection around your head and body can prevent injuries when you come back down to Earth. As the proverb says, "What goes up, must come down!"

LEARNING THE BASICS

Learning a new sport means understanding and mastering the basics and the best way to do this is to join a club. See if you can find a club in your area, or start one with your friends. You'll need to take good care of your equipment, practice a lot, and make sure you have expert help. All sports keep you healthy and active. Remember to drink plenty of water, eat well, and take breaks whenever you need to.

STAY SAFE

Photographs of extreme sports are often exciting and fun to look at, but the people pictured are usually very experienced and have practiced for years. You can expect to have a fun and exciting time if you put safety first, so turn the page to get the lowdown on a range of awesome extreme sports!

SKATEBOARDING

Skateboarding dates back to the 1950s. Many sports experts say that skateboarding originated in California, where the sport of surfing met the sport of roller-skating. This resulted in the invention of a long, flat board with four wheels attached: the skateboard! To get a skateboard moving, you stand on it with one foot and push it along with the other. Once you have some speed, you glide along with both feet on the board.

YOUR BOARD!

Many people repair their own skateboards using special tools. The surface of the board may need repainting and stickers can be used to liven up the design. You could even trade stickers with members of your skateboarding club!

WHAT'S AN "OLLIE"?

An "ollie" is a common skateboarding move in which the skateboarder steps down on the back of the board in order to lift up the front and "get air." It is named after Alan "Ollie" Gelfand, a world-famous skateboarder from California.

Skateboarders often wear specially designed shoes with shock-absorbing heel pads and flat rubber soles that grip the board well.

PRO SKATER GIRL!

Elissa Steamer has won four gold medals in women's street skate at the X Games. She started skateboarding at the age of 12.

WORLD'S LONGEST RAMP JUMP

According to the *Guinness Book of World Records*, the longest skateboard ramp jump was performed by professional skateboarder Danny Way at the 2004 X Games in Los Angeles, California. Way jumped an astonishing 78.7 feet!

Wagner Ramos is a professional skateboarder, which means he skates for money, not just for fun!

THE RIGHT GEAR

When you are skateboarding, you should always wear a helmet and knee and elbow pads for protection.

FREESTYLE SCOOTING

A scooter is a close relative of the skateboard. It is essentially a skateboard with a long handle and two narrow wheels similar to rollerblade wheels. Razor scooters got their name because they resemble an old-fashioned barber's razor, the kind with a blade that flips out from a long handle.

MOPEDS AND FOOT BIKES

"Scooter" is also a term for a moped, a two-wheeled, motorcycle-like vehicle popular in Italy. Mopeds are ideal for getting around narrow city streets. Another kind of scooter is the foot bike, a bicycle with a flat, scooter-like platform in the center. The rider pushes the bike along with one foot.

HOW TO RIDE A RAZOR SCOOTER

To ride a razor scooter, place one foot on the flat part of the scooter and use your other foot to push the scooter along. Alternatively, place your second foot behind the first and glide! Use the T-shaped handle bar to steer.

MOTORIZED SCOOTERS

Some motorized scooters look just like razor scooters, but have small engines at the back. Others, called mini scooters, stand just under 3.3 feet tall and feature T-shaped handlebars. Some people want to ban certain types of motorized scooter because they can travel up to 40 mph, but offer no protection for the rider if they collide with another vehicle.

Foot bike races take place either on roads or special tracks. Competitors can race for individual medals or as part of a team in relay caces.

To stop a razor scooter, use your foot to press down on the brake that extends over the back wheel.

RAZORS AND ROLLERBLADES

A razor scooter has narrow wheels, like those on rollerblades (above). Some scooter riders have learned to be just as agile as rollerbladers, and can perform amazing stunts.

MOUNTAIN BIKING

If you like riding your bike, and you like hiking in the woods or along rough tracks, you will probably like mountain biking. Mountain biking is just what it sounds like, riding a special bike up and down hills or mountains. Some people bike in the summer on the same mountains that are used for skiing in the winter. People also bike through woods, across deserts, or on other types of rough terrain.

WHERE TO BIKE

Wondering where to mountain bike? Ask your local librarian for information about trails that are open to mountain bikes, or find out where your nearest mountain-biking group meets.

SPECIAL GEAR

Mountain biking requires a special bike, called a mountain bike! Mountain bikes have wide, bumpy tires that grip the **trail** and keep the bike stable on rocks, roots, or muddy ground. Like other bikes, mountain bikes also have gears, which let you get more power from the bike (in low gears) or more speed (in higher gears).

On a smooth road surface, a mountain bike needs more pedal-power to go the same speed as a road bike. This is because its tires provide such good grip that they slow the bike down.

Practice is an important part of mountain biking. You'll need to practice braking, especially if you are riding up and down hills or steep slopes.

SAFETY FIRST

As with many extreme sports, a helmet and knee and elbow pads will protect you from falls or flying rocks. In the extreme version of mountain biking, called **bicycle motocross (BMX)**, participants wear padded suits, protective gloves, goggles, and shoes that grip the pedals. The full-face helmet worn by BMX riders closely resembles those used for skiing, riding motorcycles, or **snowmobiling**.

OLYMPIC GAMES

Cross-country mountain biking was first officially included in the Olympics in 1996. That year, Bart Brentjens of the Netherlands won the gold medal. He also won an Olympic bronze in 2004.

BE PREPARED!

Muddy or rocky trails can wear out both you and your bike, so it is important to carry a few essentials with you. Take a water bottle, so you don't get dehydrated, and a repair kit, in case you need to repair your bike in a remote place. Your repair kit should include a multi-tool designed to repair bikes, a patch kit for fixing flat tires, and a small pump.

X TERRAS

Three-part, multi-sport events are called triathlons (see pages 106-109). Some special triathlons, often called XTerras, involve mountain biking instead of road biking. Participants swim in a lake, go mountain biking, and then run to the finish. Form a group so you can train for an X Terra together!

In a motocross race, all riders start at the same time, and the first biker across the finish line wins.

MOTOCROSS AND BMX

Motocross is related to mountain biking, but motorcycles are ridden instead of bicycles. The gas-powered motorcycles can go much faster and cover longer distances than mountain bikes.

BMX bikes are pedal-powered racing bikes. They have smaller wheels than mountain bikes and are designed for strength.

HOLD TIGHT!

Motocross is very demanding! Riders must control a heavy motorcycle while driving as fast as possible on a rough and bumpy course.

BRAKE POWER

A mountain bike's brakes (called **cantilever brakes**) are more like motorcycle brakes than a road bike's **caliper brakes**. Cantilever brakes give you more control over how fast you come down a hill. Many experienced mountain bikers descend using a technique called feathering: gently squeezing and releasing the brake repeatedly. Feathering can prevent the wheels from locking. If your wheels lock, you can go into a spin, which could cause an injury.

Mountain biking is a great form of exercise. Pedaling uses the muscles in your legs and hips, and steering the bike strengthens your arm muscles.

IMBA

The International Mountain Bicycling Association (IMBA) is dedicated to preserving and expanding trails for mountain biking. Its members ride on trails all over the world. Check it out at: www.imba.com

SNORKELING

Snorkeling is a fun and easy extreme sport, providing you can swim! All you need to get started is a mask, a snorkel, and flippers. You can snorkel in a fresh lake, exploring the shoreline for tadpoles and frogs, or in the ocean, where you might see brightly colored fish swim by.

FLIPPERS

To swim with flippers, you'll need to learn how to do the "flutter kick." This involves kicking rapidly back and forth with your legs straight (no bending at the knees).

FUN WITH FLIPPERS

Breathing through a snorkel and swimming with a mask and flippers all at the same time may take a little while to learn. If you are a beginner, first try swimming with just the flippers to get used to the feel of them. You'll be able to go really fast!

MASK AND SNORKEL

A snorkeling mask is fun to wear because it lets you see while keeping the water out of your eyes. Breathing through the mouthpiece and the tube of the snorkel takes practice. Don't forget to hold your breath if you dive under the water because water will go down the tube! You will need to blow the water back out of the tube when you come back up to the surface.

The rubber rim of a snorkel mask fits tightly around the face so that water can't get in.

SCUBA DIVING

Scuba diving is a sport for adults. Wearing special equipment, scuba divers can swim deep under the sea and can stay under water for long periods of time. Sometimes they are hired to look for treasure or shipwrecks.

DIVING DEEP

Scuba divers carry **oxygen tanks** on their backs for underwater breathing and wear wetsuits, rubber gloves, and rubber boots. They may also wear a headlamp because it's very dark deep in the ocean!

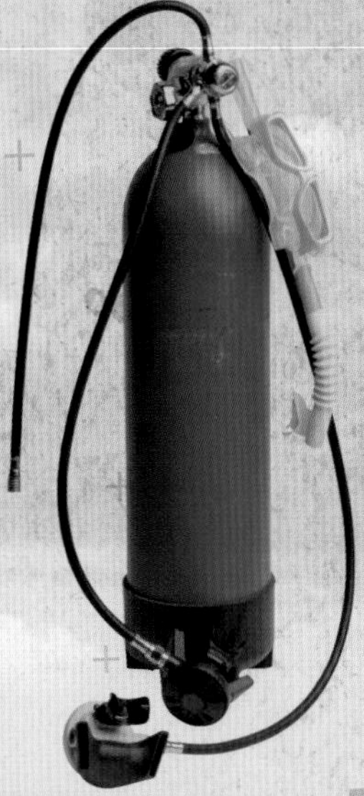

WORLD RECORD

According to the *Guinness Book of World Records*, the deepest scuba dive was achieved in June 2005 by South African scuba diver Nuno Gomes. Nuno dived to a depth of 1,044.13 feet. That is almost equal to the height of the Eiffel Tower in Paris, France!

In shallow coastal waters, a snorkeler can see all kinds of wonderful things, such as these starfish off the coast of Honeymoon Island, Palau, in the Pacific Ocean.

KITING

When you think of flying a kite, you may think of a simple diamond-shaped piece of plastic, a few wooden sticks, and a ball of string. But kite surfing and other kite sports are far more extreme than that! Competitive kite flying is growing in popularity. In the USA, Germany, Japan, and Thailand (among other countries) people fly kites more than 79 feet long.

KITE VARIETIES

There are many different types of kites, including single-string kites, which you may have flown in a field or on a beach; stunt kites, which are designed to do tricks or special maneuvers; and power kites, which have enough power to pull surfers across the ocean or snowboarders across snow.

STACK

STACK stands for Sport Team and Competitive Kiting, an organization that tries to bring together anyone who loves the sport of kiting. Its members compete in Individual, Pairs, Team, and Trick-flying kite competitions all over the world.

KITESURFING

To kitesurf, you use a large kite to pull yourself across water on a wakeboard. Experts are able to perform amazing jumps.

FESTIVALS AND COMPETITIONS

One easy way to become familiar with kiting is to go to a competition or festival. There are kite competitions for speed and design, and festivals that celebrate sport kites, **box kites**, foils (soft, semi-inflated kites used for kitesurfing and snowkiting), and deltas (arrow-shaped kites used for stunts). A major kiting event is held each year in Washington, D.C. It includes a kite design competition which is judged based on visual appeal and handling, and trick flying competitions.

To kitesurf, you need to be a strong swimmer and a skilled kite-flyer.

SNOWKITING

Snowkiting is similar to kitesurfing, but instead combines a kite and a snowboard. Check out the Swiss Snowkiting School's Web site: www.snowkiting.ch (To get the English-language version, click on "english" in the black bar at the top of the home page.)

SURFING

Surfing may have its roots in the ancient cultures of Polynesia and Tahiti. It was witnessed in the late 1770s by explorer Captain James Cook who saw the native people in Hawaii riding waves on wooden boards. Today's boards, made from a special kind of **resin-coated** plastic, include **surfboards**, paipo (short boards), and round **skimmers**.

Skysurfers wear parachutes on their backs. The chutes carry them safely back to the ground after surfing for a while.

THE BIGGEST WAVES

Major surfing centers have popped up along the Pacific and Atlantic coasts. These coasts have some of the world's biggest waves. Australia, California, and Hawaii all have strong surfing communities. By some estimates, there are 20 million surfers worldwide. The sport is exciting to watch, especially the world-class surfers, who tackle the biggest waves the ocean can produce.

TAKE TO THE AIR

Surfing brings together a body, a board, and a wave. Skysurfing combines a body, a board, and the air. Skysurfers jump out of a plane and ride air currents using a board strapped to their feet! Only highly trained professionals are able to do this sport.

SURF ART

Surfboard artist Drew Brophy of California is extremely well known among musicians. In fact, his painted surfboards sell for thousands of dollars! Drew says his designs are inspired by the ocean, surfing, and nature.

SURFING VS. BODYBOARDING

Watching the world's best surfers and learning how to surf are two very different things! Learning to surf (or windsurf, which adds a sail and apparatus to the board) requires time and patience. You may prefer bodyboarding, which is like surfing while lying down on a 3.3-foot long board (also called a boogie board). You could also try riding a round, thin board called a skimmer. To ride a skimboard, you run toward the water from the beach. Then you jump on the board with both feet and glide through the shallow water.

WORLD RECORD HOLDER

According to the *Guinness Book of World Records*, Mike Stewart has won 9 world championships in bodyboarding and has won the Pipiline Bodysurfing Classic 13 times. (Pipeline is a famous Hawaiian wave venue.)

While lying on the board, a surfer first paddles out to sea. When a wave comes in, the surfer stands up on his or her feet. Some surfers prefer to crouch on one knee first to make sure both feet are in the right position before standing.

SURF LINGO

Surfing has a language and culture all its own. In California, for instance, "cooking" means a great wave and "noodled" means exhausted. "Wipe out" means to fall off the board, which is when you don't want to meet a "landlord" (a great white shark). "Hang ten" refers to a move in which you have all ten toes on the nose (front) of the board.

KNEEBOARDING

Kneeboarding and wakeboarding are great extreme water sports. These sports require the proper equipment: a good teacher, a snug life jacket, and a powerboat. When kneeboarding, you are pulled behind a boat while kneeling on a board. When wakeboarding, you are also pulled behind a boat, but you stand sideways on a board resembling a snowboard. It's fun to take part, but fun to go and watch your friends, too!

Wakeboards have to be very strong. They have to withstand pounding as their riders jump over the waves created behind the boat.

WATERSKIING

Both kneeboarding and wakeboarding are related to waterskiing, in which you are pulled behind a powerboat while standing on wide, flat skis. Waterskiing has a long history and is an Olympic sport. Check it out at www.usawaterski.org

When he's not barefoot waterskiing, Keith St. Onge likes cold-weather sports such as hockey and skiing.

BAREFOOTING

Barefoot waterskiing involves skiing on water using your bare feet! Keith St. Onge is two time World Barefoot Skiing Overall Champion. He started waterskiing at the age of 10 and has had years of experience, so don't try any of his tricks at home!

WATERSKIING VS. SNOW SKIING

Waterskiing is different from snow skiing in several ways. The skis used for waterskiing are wider. You do not usually wear boots while waterskiing because you need to be able to release your feet quickly if you fall in the water. Finally, snow skiers don't need to wear life jackets!

Many people find kneeboarding easier than waterskiing. Rather than having to balance on two skis, you simply kneel on a large board and let the boat pull you along.

ROCK CLIMBING

Rock climbing is a fun and challenging sport that can be done outdoors on real rocks or inside on climbing walls. The sport requires good upper body strength because you use your arms to pull yourself up the rocks. Beginners wear a harness designed to catch them if they fall.

WHY CLIMB A MOUNTAIN?

What makes people want to climb mountains? Sir Edmund Hillary, one of the first two men to reach the summit of Mount Everest, is reported to have said, "It is not the mountain we conquer, but ourselves." Even if you're not climbing Everest, it's fun to go hiking with friends.

INDOOR ROCK CLIMBING

Indoor climbing walls have handholds made from rubber or plastic. These allow climbers to hold on as they go up. But what goes up must come down, which is why the harness is important. Once a climber reaches the top, a trained professional holding onto ropes at the bottom guides the climber safely down again.

Rock climbers wear a padded harness that loops around the waist and legs. Safety ropes attach to the harness.

OUTDOOR ROCK CLIMBING

On outdoor rock faces, there are usually no artificial handholds to help you up. Instead, climbers must grip cracks and ledges in the rock. Special shoes provide extra grip.

Rock climbers don't just need to be physically strong. They also need to have a positive mental attitude. Climbers need to stay relaxed and confident because some climbs can take many hours.

HIGH RISKS

Climbing mountains, rockfaces, or ice formations (such as ice walls, ice slopes, or **glaciers**) requires special equipment, including **crampons**, **ice axes**, **nuts**, **cams**, and ropes. It should only be done by highly trained professionals who know their equipment, are familiar with the territory, and understand the risks involved.

KAYAKING

If you like the water, kayaking may be the extreme sport for you. A kayak is a lightweight, enclosed boat that is paddled on lakes, rivers, or in the ocean. To move the boat, you dip a two-sided paddle into the water on each side of the kayak, one side at a time. Some kayaks are designed for one person, others for two.

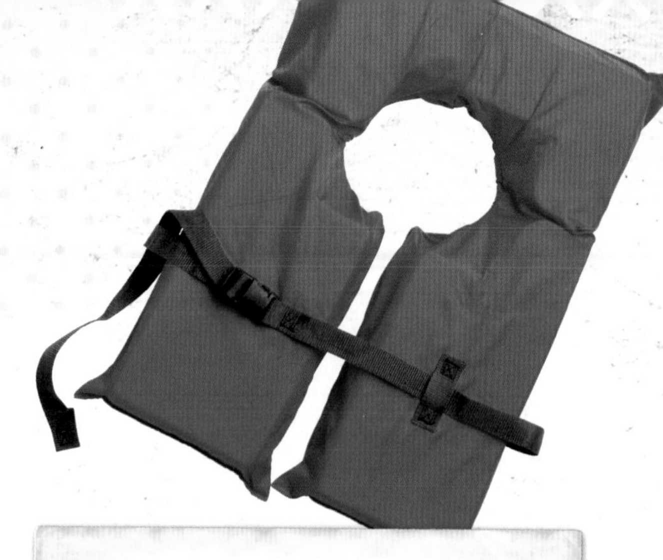

LIFE JACKETS

Many states require children to wear life jackets whenever they are in a boat. Life jackets are just as important as seat belts, so don't leave home without one!

SPLASHING AROUND!

Kayaking is closely related to **canoeing** and **rafting**, both of which are fun boating sports. In the US and Canada, as well as parts of South America and New Zealand, small boats called Sunfish are popular.

Sunfish are great sailing boats for children because they're lightweight and easy for one person to sail alone.

WHITE WATER KAYAKING

The most extreme version of kayaking is white water kayaking. You need to be highly trained for this sport. The kayak gets maneuvered through rough and unpredictable "white water" **rapids**, which are very fast flowing. The sport is exciting (even scary) to watch because it can be dangerous. It is definitely not for beginners!

WHITE WATER RAFTING

The most extreme version of rafting is called white water rafting. It requires a trained instructor, a large **inflatable boat**, and a group of friends. The aim is to paddle the boat along a fast-flowing river. Everyone wears life jackets and helmets in case they fall out of the raft.

White water kayakers can choose the difficulty of the river in which they kayak. A Class VI (six) river is the most difficult and dangerous to navigate. A Class I (one) is the easiest.

ULTIMATE FRISBEE

Players can expect to run several miles during a game of Ultimate. .

Ultimate Frisbee, or "Ultimate" for short, is a fast-moving team sport. It is sometimes compared to football or soccer but it has a unique feature: instead of a ball, players pass a Frisbee back and forth. It's easy to form a team with friends and play against other people!

THE JOKE THAT BECAME A SPORT

Ultimate was created in 1968 by Joel Silver at Columbia High School in New Jersey. Joel asked his school for an Ultimate Frisbee team to be created as a joke! He certainly could not have foreseen how popular it would become.

GET IN THE GAME

Ultimate is played by two teams of seven, on a field that is a similar size to a football field. The last 60 feet on both ends are called "endzones." A goal is scored when you throw the Frisbee to a player on your team who is in the endzone your team is attacking. Players are not allowed to run with the disc, so you need to come to a halt when you catch the disc and then pass it on.

NO REFEREES!

Ultimate is a "non-contact" sport, which means players don't come into physical contact during the game. Players "self-referee," which means that fouls and conflicts are resolved between players, rather than by a third-party referee. Because the rules are simple, this is a great sport to pick up quickly.

DID YOU KNOW?!

Variations of Ultimate include Beach Ultimate, Freestyle and Double Disc Court, in which two Frisbees are used.

MULTI-SPORT EVENTS

Multi-sport events are sporting events that combine more than one kind of sports. There are many different types of multi-sport events. A "triathlon" combines swimming, cycling, and running. ("Tri" is from the Greek word for three.) The winter sport of "biathlon" combines cross-country skiing and rifle shooting (although the term "biathlon" can be used to describe any two-sport event). In a "duathlon," an athlete runs, bikes, and then runs again.

The swimming part of a junior triathlon can take place in a lake or in a pool.

TRIATHLON WORLD CHAMPION

Alistair Brownlee of the UK won the men's 2011 triathlon World Championship and won gold in the 2012 Olympic Games. Alistair finished the 0.9-mile swim, 24.9-mile bike ride, and a 6.2-mile run in 1 hour, 46 minutes and 25 seconds.

ALL-AROUND SKILLS

You may be good at swimming, biking, and running, but triathlon requires another skill, too. A triathlete must also be able to change clothes and/or equipment quickly and efficiently at "transitions," the time between stages. Triathletes need three sets of equipment: goggles and cap for swimming; bike and helmet for biking; and sneakers for running. Keeping it all organized is very important because the quicker the transition time, the faster the finishing time!

TRANSITION AREA

The transition area is the place to which the athlete returns after each leg of the triathlon. After swimming, for instance, the competitor must take off his or her goggles and cap and quickly put on cycling shorts, gloves, shoes, and a helmet.

After finishing the swim, triathletes run to their bikes, where they put on shoes and a helmet before cycling off.

Some athletes wear special suits for all three stages of a triathlon.

CHOICE OF EVENTS

Each year in Oklahoma, competitors can compete in an event called a half REDMAN (swim 1.2 mi, bike 56 mi, and run 13 mi; a full REDMAN, which is twice as far, the distance of a full **marathon**); or do the Aqua Bike event (swimming and cycling).

KID STAR

Sara McLarty has been the U.S. IronKids champion four times. She lives in Colorado Springs, Colorado, where the Olympic triathlon team trains. Sara first became an IronKids champion at the age of 10.

Before attempting the swimming portion of the race, triathletes do some warm-up exercises and then stretch their arms to give their muscles greater flexibility.

The run is sometimes the hardest part of a triathlon because competitors' bodies are already tired from the biking and swimming portions.

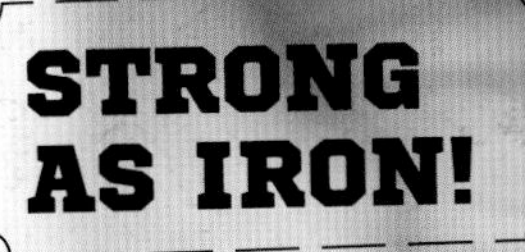

One of the most famous triathlon events is called the Ironman (in which women also compete). Competitors in this grueling event swim, bike, and run the same distances as a full REDMAN. Children can compete in their own version of the race called IronKids. Junior triathlon distances might include a 137-yard swim, a 4.9-mile bike ride, and a 1.6-mile run. To find out more, go to: www.ironkids.com

GLOSSARY

aerial A style of downhill skiing in which skiers perform jumps, flips, twists, and other moves.

aerodynamic Something with a streamlined shape that allows wind or air to flow over it easily, making it go faster.

amateur A person who plays a sport for pleasure, rather than being paid to do so.

Arctic The icy region around the North Pole.

artificial snow Snow made by a machine.

asphalt A smooth, paved surface.

attack, attacking The players who play in a forward position near the opponent's goal and attempt to score.

base Square marker used in baseball to mark three of the four points of the baseball diamond. (Home plate is the fourth.)

baseman (baseball) A fielding position; the first baseman plays on first base, the second baseman on second base, etc.

bindings Devices that hold boots to skis or a snowboard. Downhill skiers insert their boots toe-first into the bindings, then put their heels down to snap the bindings closed around the boots. Snowboarders place their whole boots into the bindings, which have straps over the toes and ankles that they tighten by hand.

BMX (bicycle motocross) A sport in which special mountain bikes are raced over rough ground around a hilly course.

bobsled A long fiberglass or metal sled with two sets of steel runners. Bobsleds are big enough for two or four athletes to sit inside.

boogie board A smaller, shorter version of a surfboard ridden in shallow water.

box kite A classic type of kite in the shape of a rectangular box.

bump (volleyball) To hit the ball to another player on your team using both forearms held close together.

caliper brakes A type of bicycle brake found on road bikes. Caliper brakes attach above the wheel and squeeze together on either side of the wheel rim to slow the bike down.

cams (mountaineering) Cams are grooved, wheel-like devices with handles. They are inserted into cracks in the rock and attached to climbing ropes. If placed at frequent intervals up the rockface, they will stop a climber from falling very far.

canoeing Paddling a canoe, a long, narrow boat with pointed ends like a kayak, but with an open top.

cantilever brakes A type of bicycle brake found on mountain bikes. Cantilever brakes attach next to the wheel and are more powerful than caliper brakes.

catcher (baseball) The player who catches the ball thrown by the pitcher.

caterpillar track A steel band looped around the wheels of a vehicle such as a snow cat. It allows the vehicle to travel over rough ground or across snow and ice.

coach An instructor who works with players to improve their skills.

conversion (rugby) A successful kick at the goalposts after a try has been awarded.

conveyor belt A continuous moving band that moves things from one place to another.

crampon An iron plate with spikes that gets attached to boots to give grip when walking on ice.

cue ball The white ball used to hit other balls in snooker and pool.

defense, defending The defensive team, or the players who stay near their own goal and defend it when the other team attempts to score.

deflect To block or hit the ball so that it changes direction.

dig (volleyball) A pass made from close to the floor after receiving a spike. You hit the ball to a teammate using the inside of the forearms.

driving range A place for golfers to practice hitting and driving.

drop goal (rugby) A goal scored by dropping the ball and kicking it over the crossbar of the goalposts.

drop-kick (rugby) A rugby move in which the player drops the ball and kicks it just as it touches the ground.

fielder A player whose job is to catch or stop the ball and return it.

FIFA The letters stand for the Fédération Internationale de Football Association, French for the International Federation of Association Football.

GLOSSARY

figure skating Performing moves such as jumps or spins on ice, either alone or with a partner.

forward A player who tries to score on the opposing team's goal.

foul To make an illegal move or to break a rule of the game.

gain possession To get control of the ball from the other team.

game (tennis) A match is made up of a series of games. A game is won when one player, or pair, scores at least four points and is more than one point ahead of the opponent(s). (The first point is called 15, the second is 30, the third is 40, and 40-all is called deuce. The next person to score has the "advantage." If the player with the advantage wins the next point, he or she wins the game. If he or she loses it, the score goes back to deuce.)

glacier A large body of ice moving very slowly down a valley.

green The large, level area of short grass on which lawn bowls is played.

home plate (baseball) The base that runners must reach to score a run.

ice ax An ax used by mountaineerers for cutting footholds in the ice. One end is hooked and has a serrated edge (like a steak knife).

inflatable boat A boat that is filled with air in order to float.

iron A type of golf club generally used for accurate shots taken between the tee and the green.

K point The distance to aim for when ski jumping, marked by the K line on the landing strip.

lava Hot, molten volcanic rock.

league A group of sports teams who compete among themselves.

Little League A U.S. organization that manages baseball and softball leagues for children all around the world.

luge A type of sled with two runners, called steels, and a flat seat on which the rider lies down.

marathon A road race covering a distance of 26.2 miles.

Masters A major golf tournament played each year in the USA.

match (tennis) A tennis match consists of between two and five sets. A set includes at least six games.

midfielder (soccer) A player who mostly plays in the center of the field.

mogul A steep mound or ridge of snow on a ski slope.

motocross A sport in which a motorcycle is raced over rough or hilly terrain.

muscles Tissue in the body that controls the movement of body parts.

nuts (mountaineering) Metal wedges that can be inserted into cracks in the rock. Safety ropes are attached to the nuts, to stop a climber from falling very far.

Open A competition (as in the U.S. Open in golf and tennis) which nationally top-rated athletes, either amateur or professional, may enter.

oxygen tank A tank that holds oxygen and is used when swimming underwater or mountaineering in high altitudes.

passing (rugby and basketball) To toss or throw the ball to another player.

penalty box A place where ice hockey players sit when taken out of play for breaking the rules.

penalty kick When a player breaks a rule, the other team is awarded a penalty kick at the goal to try to score.

pitcher The baseball player who throws, or pitches, the ball over home plate towards the batter and the catcher. The batter tries to hit the ball before it reaches the catcher.

professional A person who earns money by playing a sport.

puck (ice hockey) A small, thick disc that players try to hit into the goals. Made of smooth rubber, it glides easily across the ice.

putter A flat-sided golf club used on the green to hit the ball into the hole.

qualifying matches Games played in the two years before the World Cup to decide which teams will take part.

quarterback The leader of a team in football. He or she suggests what tactics the players should use.

GLOSSARY

rafting To ride an inflatable raft down a river, often over rapids.

rapids Fast-moving parts of a river, where the water tumbles over and between rocks. Rapids are also known as "white water" because the bubbles make the water look white.

reserves Extra players on a team who may be called in to play if another player is injured, tired, or not playing well.

resin A liquid substance that hardens; artificial resins are used in some plastics. Natural resin is found in the gum of some trees.

rink A frozen surface for ice hockey or skating, kept frozen by machines.

rounders A game in which two teams of nine players take turns batting and fielding the ball, and running around four posts to score rounders.

ruck (rugby) A battle for possession of the ball once it has been dropped by a tackled player.

runners (football) Players who run with the ball. For example, a receiver's job is to get into the open so he or she can catch a forward pass from the quarterback and then run with the ball; or the two running backs, who are handed the ball by the quarterback and then run with it.

scrum (rugby) A type of play used to restart the action. The forwards on both teams interlock arms to form a tunnel into which the ball is tossed.

scuba The letters "scuba" stand for Self Contained Underwater Breathing Apparatus. It is the name given to part of the gear used by underwater divers.

serving (volleyball) To start the play for a new point by hitting the ball over the net.

set (tennis) A tennis match consists of between two and five sets. To win a set, a player or team has to win at least six games, and at least two games more than their opponent(s). For example, six games to four or seven games to five.

shooting circle The semicircular area in front of a field hockey goal. Shots on goal must be made from within the circle.

set (volleyball) To hit the ball up into the air using both hands, often done so a teammate can slam it over the net.

sidelines The lines on a field that mark the edges of the playing area.

skateboard A board measuring about 29 inches long and about 8 inches wide with two wheels at each end.

skimmer A round, thin board with no fin. It is about half the length and thickness of a surfboard.

slalom To move in a zigzag formation between obstacles.

snowmobiling A sport in which you race a motorized sled across ice and snow.

softball A game similar to baseball that uses a larger ball and is played on a smaller diamond.

striker (soccer) An attacking player who tries to kick the ball into the goal.

surfboard A long, flat board about 9 feet long and 2 feet wide, used by surfers for riding waves in the ocean.

tackling A way of gaining possession of the ball by taking it away from another player.

tee, tee off The tee is the place on a golf course from which the ball is struck (teed off) at the beginning of play for each hole.

terrain Land used for activities such as mountain biking or hiking.

trail A path used for sports such as walking, hiking, and mountain biking. In snowboarding and snow skiing, the path that takes you from the top of the mountain to the bottom.

triathlon A multi-sport event that combines swimming, biking (road or mountain), and running.

try line A goal line on a rugby field.

touch (rugby) The ball is said to be "in touch" if it crosses the touchline (sideline).

UFO Unidentified Flying Object.

wood A type of golf club used to hit the ball off the tee or for long distances.

World Series The annual competition between the top two Major League Baseball teams.

X Games An international competition similar to the Olympics that includes sports such as skateboarding.

INDEX

INDEX